# The Washington Monument

## CORNERSTONES OF FREEDOM

### SECOND SERIES

Elaine Landau

**Children's Press®**
A Division of Scholastic Inc.
New York • Toronto • London • Auckland • Sydney
Mexico City • New Delhi • Hong Kong
Danbury, Connecticut

Photographs © 2004: AP/Wide World Photos/Ron Edmonds: 41;
Bridgeman Art Library International Ltd., London/New York/Temple of
Amun, Luxor, Egypt: 31; Brown Brothers: 4, 8; Corbis Images: 3, 16,
19, 24, 26, 29, 37, 38, 44 top left and right (Bettmann), 40 bottom
(Reuters), 17 (Paul A. Souders), 13 left, 14, 25, 33, 36, 44 bottom; Folio,
Inc.: 40 top (Tal McBride), 21, 45 top (Robert C. Shafer);
Hulton|Archive/Getty Images: 28; ImageState: cover bottom (Sharon
Jacobs), 39 (Andre Jenny); Library of Congress: 27 (Francis Hacker), cover
top (via SODA), 23; National Archives and Records Administration/George
Washington Bicentennial Commission via SODA: 6 left; North Wind
Picture Archives: 12, 18, 32; Omni-Photo Communications/Folio: 9;
PictureHistory.com: 11; Robertstock.com: 34, 45 bottom (R. Kord), 5;
Stock Montage, Inc.: 13 right , 20; U.S. Capitol Historical Society,
Washington, DC/via SODA: 6 right, 7.

Library of Congress Cataloging-in-Publication Data
Landau, Elaine.
  The Washington Monument / Elaine Landau.
      p. cm. — (Cornerstones of freedom. Second series)
Summary: Tells the story of the Washington Monument, giving information
on the nation's first president whom the monument honors and describing
the process of designing and building the monument.
  Includes bibliographical references (p. ) and index.
    ISBN 0-516-24238-5
    1. Washington Monument (Washington, D.C.)—Juvenile literature.
2. Washington (D.C.)—Buildings, structures, etc.—Juvenile literature.
3. Washington, George, 1732–1799—Juvenile literature. [1. Washington
Monument (Washington, D.C.) 2. Washington, George, 1732–1799.
3. National monuments.] I. Title. II. Series.
F203.4.W3L36 2003
917.53—dc22

                                            2003016942

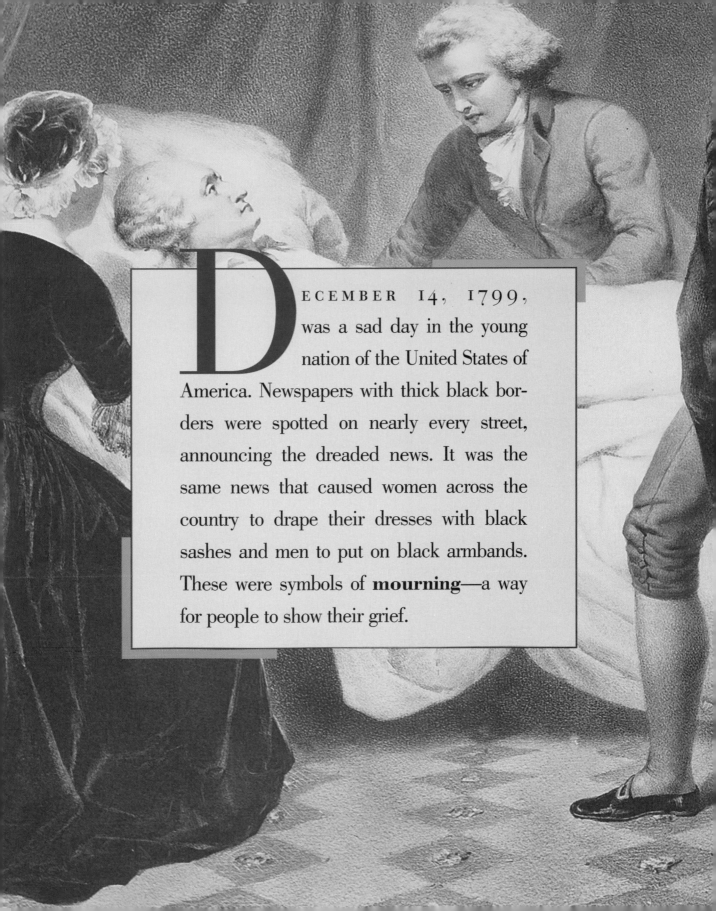

DECEMBER 14, 1799, was a sad day in the young nation of the United States of America. Newspapers with thick black borders were spotted on nearly every street, announcing the dreaded news. It was the same news that caused women across the country to drape their dresses with black sashes and men to put on black armbands. These were symbols of **mourning**—a way for people to show their grief.

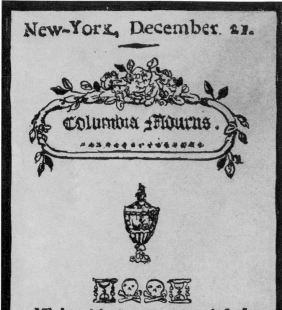

Columbia Mourns.

IT is with the deepest grief that we announce to the public the death of our *most diftinguifhed* fellow-citizen *Lieut. General George Wafhington.* He died at Mount Vernon on Saturday evening, the 13th inf of an inflammatory affection of the throat, which put a period to his exiftence in 23 hours.

The grief which we fuffer on this truly mournful occafion, would be in fome degree aleviated, if we poffeffed abilities to do juftice to the merits of this *illuftrious benefactor of mankind*; but, confcious of our inferiority, we fhrink from the fublimity of the fubject.

**Across the country, news articles sadly announced the death of George Washington.**

That day, it seemed as if the whole nation was in mourning. George Washington, the nation's first president, was dead. Dying of a throat infection at his Mount Vernon estate in Virginia, his last words were, "'Tis well."

Most Americans would have agreed with him. Things had been going well for the new and growing country. The United States was a nation with a bright future. While serving in its highest office, Washington had done much to help set the country on the right course. Now the nation was left to deal with the loss of a much-loved statesman and leader.

## FROM THE START

Through the years, Washington's words and actions had shown Americans the meaning of **patriotism**. Some people doubted that the American Revolution would have been won without his leadership. Few of the colonists had military experience, and there was little money with which to buy weapons and ammunition to fight the British. Nevertheless, Washington took on the challenge of leading the colonists in battle. In 1775, he was appointed commander-in-chief of the raggedy, poorly trained fighting force known as the Continental army. After accepting the command, he modestly noted, "I beg it be remembered by every

Washington's strength and leadership during the American Revolution inspired the Continental army to victory. He is shown here directing the Battle of Princeton.

gentleman in this room, that . . . I do not think myself equal to the command I am honored with."

As it turned out, Washington was more than worthy of the command. Even with inexperienced soldiers and serious supply shortages, Washington led his men to victory.

When the fighting was over, some of his troops wanted him to be crowned the king of the United States. They respected and admired Washington and thought he would rule the United States wisely and fairly.

**More than anyone else, George Washington was responsible for shaping the fundamental beliefs and values of our country.**

However, Washington scoffed at the idea. He had fought to help create a nation in which equality reigned, not kings and queens. Washington believed that Americans were capable of governing themselves. That was his dream for the country.

While Washington had hoped to retire from public life after the war, he knew there was more work to be done. The United States needed to build a firm foundation. It was

especially important that a constitution be put in place. The Articles of Confederation, the country's first constitution, left the government with few powers. It could not tax its citizens or control its borders. Washington knew that a weak government would have trouble protecting the nation in the future.

So during the summer of 1787, a Constitutional Convention was held in Philadelphia, Pennsylvania. Its purpose was to create a constitution that would last through the years. Washington agreed to go to the Convention as a delegate, or representative, from Virginia. After arriving, the other delegates chose him to take charge of this historic meeting.

★  ★  ★  ★

Washington was inaugurated, or sworn in, as president on April 30, 1789. He took the oath of office on the balcony of Federal Hall in New York.

The new Constitution required the nation to have a president. It was widely believed that Washington was the best man for the job. Electors from every state **unanimously** selected him. Washington accepted the offer. In 1789, he began to serve the first of two terms in office.

As president, Washington strengthened the military and the country's national banking system. He set the young nation on a course that would eventually lead it to become one of the world's most successful republics. In a republic, the people elect representatives to manage the government. That was Washington's hope for the United States, and he tried to mold the government in this way.

* * * *

Washington turned down the offer to serve a third term as president. By then, he was about sixty years old and had already served the nation for a number of years. At that point, he longed to spend time at his beloved Mount Vernon home. In his farewell address, Washington urged all Americans "to properly estimate the immense value of your national Union." In saying that, he reminded his fellow citizens that their true strength was in their unity as a nation.

Washington was admired and respected when he died. Citizens of the young nation knew they had lost a great leader.

## MOUNT VERNON

George Washington's favorite place was his Mount Vernon estate. Much of the estate's 8,000 acres (3,240 hectares) was used as farmland, but it also included a large house, groves of trees, and a lovely garden. Washington once said, "I can truly say I had rather be at home at Mount Vernon with a friend or two about me than to be attended at the seat of government by the officers of State and the representatives of every power in Europe."

Today, Mount Vernon is the most visited historic home in the United States, after the White House.

# A LASTING TRIBUTE

George Washington's death plunged the country into mourning. Washington's funeral took place in Virginia, and people around the country held services to honor his memory. Numerous poems and stories were written to praise him. For months following Washington's death, stores could not keep enough black armbands in stock to meet the demand. In death, Washington's reputation grew even greater. People began to think of him as a national hero.

Americans wanted to honor the man who had done so much for the country. Many thought that a monument would serve as a lasting **tribute** to him. A monument is a statue or building put up to honor a person or to remind people of an important event.

The idea of honoring Washington with a monument was not new. Even before his death, there was talk of erecting a statue of the man known as the "Father of His Country." In 1783, the Continental Congress (the early Congress made up of delegates from the colonies) proposed that a statue of Washington on his horse be built wherever the Congress's permanent home was to be established. The statue was never erected, in part because the government did not become firmly rooted in Washington, D.C., until 1800.

After that, other obstacles to the creation of the monument arose. When French engineer Pierre-Charles L'Enfant was hired to design the nation's capital, his plans included a

Members of the Continental Congress discussed building a statue of George Washington as early as 1783.

Washington's statue was put on hold as the capital city was constructed.

statue of Washington on a horse. Building the capital, however, took a great deal of money. At the time, there wasn't enough to go around. It was clear that the statue would have to wait until more money became available.

Washington's death brought on new pressures to act. The American people wanted their leaders to do something to honor him. A group of congressmen met ten days after Washington died to discuss how to proceed. At the time, Virginia representative John Marshall suggested that a fancy tomb for Washington be built in the U.S. Capitol building

## A MUCH-HONORED STATESMAN

As time passed, George Washington would be honored many times in different ways. The nation's capital, as well as one of the states, was named after him. Numerous streets, counties, and universities across the country are named after the first president as well.

in Washington, D.C. But Washington's family was not in favor of this idea. They had already buried him and refused to move his body. The proposal faced other problems, too. Any new project had to be put on hold because of the lack of funds.

## THE PEOPLE TAKE OVER

Many years passed before work on creating a fitting **memorial** for George Washington finally began. In 1833, a year after the one hundredth anniversary of Washington's birth, an interested group of citizens got together to take over the task. The newly formed organization was known as the Washington National Monument Society.

After Washington's death, Virginia representative John Marshall proposed that a tomb be erected within the Capitol.

This certificate from the Washington National Monument Society was issued around 1849. It contains the printed signatures of various members of the society.

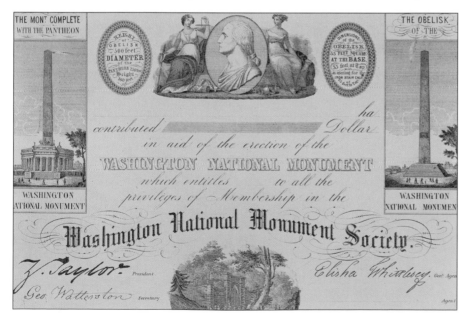

13

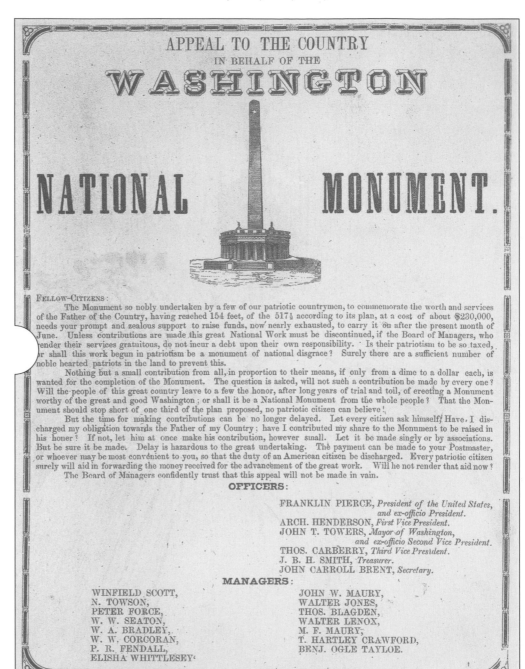

# APPEAL TO THE COUNTRY
## IN BEHALF OF THE
# WASHINGTON
# NATIONAL          MONUMENT.

FELLOW-CITIZENS:

The Monument so nobly undertaken by a few of our patriotic countrymen, to commemorate the worth and services of the Father of the Country, having reached 154 feet, of the 517½ according to its plan, at a cost of about $230,000, needs your prompt and zealous support to raise funds, now nearly exhausted, to carry it on after the present month of June. Unless contributions are made this great National Work must be discontinued, if the Board of Managers, who render their services gratuitous, do not incur a debt upon their own responsibility. Is their patriotism to be so taxed, or shall this work begun in patriotism be a monument of national disgrace? Surely there are a sufficient number of noble hearted patriots in the land to prevent this.

Nothing but a small contribution from all, in proportion to their means, if only from a dime to a dollar each, is wanted for the completion of the Monument. The question is asked, will not such a contribution be made by every one? Will the people of this great country leave to a few the honor, after long years of trial and toil, of erecting a Monument worthy of the great and good Washington; or shall it be a National Monument from the whole people? That the Monument should stop short of one third of the plan proposed, no patriotic citizen can believe.

But the time for making contributions can be no longer delayed. Let every citizen ask himself, Have I discharged my obligation towards the Father of my Country; have I contributed my share to the Monument to be raised in his honor? If not, let him at once make his contribution, however small. Let it be made singly or by associations. But be sure it be made. Delay is hazardous to the great undertaking. The payment can be made to your Postmaster, or whoever may be most convenient to you, so that the duty of an American citizen be discharged. Every patriotic citizen surely will aid in forwarding the money received for the advancement of the great work. Will he not render that aid now?

The Board of Managers confidently trust that this appeal will not be made in vain.

### OFFICERS:

FRANKLIN PIERCE, *President of the United States, and ex-officio President.*
ARCH. HENDERSON, *First Vice President.*
JOHN T. TOWERS, *Mayor of Washington, and ex-officio Second Vice President.*
THOS. CARBERRY, *Third Vice President.*
J. B. H. SMITH, *Treasurer.*
JOHN CARROLL BRENT, *Secretary.*

### MANAGERS:

WINFIELD SCOTT,
N. TOWSON,
PETER FORCE,
W. W. SEATON,
W. A. BRADLEY,
W. W. CORCORAN,
P. R. FENDALL,
ELISHA WHITTLESEY.

JOHN W. MAURY,
WALTER JONES,
THOS. BLAGDEN,
WALTER LENOX,
M. F. MAURY,
T. HARTLEY CRAWFORD,
BENJ. OGLE TAYLOE.

**Posters such as this one appealed to the American public to raise funds for the construction of the monument.**

14

John Marshall headed this group. Although Marshall had wanted to build a tomb for Washington more than thirty years earlier, he and the other group members were open to new ideas.

As always, money was still a problem. Before any suggestions for a monument could be considered, the group needed to raise cash to pay for it. To spread the word about the monument, the society put notices in newspapers, journals, and bulletins. It sent representatives to churches, businesses, and various clubs and social organizations to ask people to help.

By 1836, the society had collected about $28,000. Its members were ready to start. At that point, no one knew what form the monument would take or who would design it. Nevertheless, the Society wanted the finished product to meet certain standards. These included being able to "blend stupendousness [tremendous size] with elegance" and "be of such magnitude and beauty as to be an object of pride to the American people." The monument was also to be 100 percent American. As the group put it, "Its [the monument's] material is intended to be wholly American, and be made of marble and granite brought from each state, that each state may participate in the glory of contributing material as well as funds to its construction."

In 1836, the Washington National Monument Society held a contest to find the best design for the monument. American artists and builders were invited to submit their ideas. The winner was an **architect** from South Carolina named Robert Mills.

Although Mills designed many public buildings, the Washington Monument would become his best-known structure.

# A GRAND MONUMENT

Many people thought Mills was an excellent choice for the project. Mills was the first professionally trained architect born in the United States. Before entering the design contest, he had worked as an architect in such cities as Philadelphia, Baltimore, and Washington, D.C.

Mills had recently been appointed Architect of Public Buildings for Washington, D.C. He knew every street and waterway in the area. He had designed a number of important public structures in the capital city. Mills was also accustomed to working on tributes to George Washington. He'd already designed a monument—a statue of Washington on top of a tall column—in Baltimore, Maryland.

The monument Mills proposed for the capital was considerably grander than the one he designed for Baltimore. The centerpiece of his tribute to Washington was a 600-foot (183-meter) obelisk. An obelisk is a tapering four-sided pillar or column. The obelisk Mills wanted for the monument would have a nearly flat top. At the base of the obelisk, Mills planned to have a circular building designed to look like an ancient Greek temple. A statue of Washington in an ancient **chariot** drawn by six horses would rest on top of the building, which would be surrounded by a circle of columns called a colonnade.

In honor of Washington's leadership during the American Revolution, thirty other statues would be placed within the monument's colonnade. These would depict men who

Robert Mills' monument in Baltimore was completed in 1829. It was the first major monument to be built in honor of George Washington.

**This illustration shows Mills's early design for the Washington Monument.**

fought bravely alongside him during the war. The finished product was to be a magnificent structure that would leave people in awe. It's likely that the proposed price tag for it would have had the same effect. The estimated cost for the monument was $1,250,000.

Work on the monument did not begin right away. Although the Washington National Monument Society had approved Mills's design, doubts about it soon came up. Some people felt the design was overly **complex**. Nearly everyone felt the cost was too high as well. Over the next few years, Mills submitted simpler versions of his original design to the society. At the same time, society members continued their fund-raising efforts. They knew that even a simpler design would cost far more than they had anticipated.

It wasn't until 1848 that work on a simpler monument could begin. By then, the Washington National Monument Society had collected $87,000. There were still questions about the monument's final form and design. For example, the group was not sure about the temple-style building and colonnade at the monument's base. So, construction began with the obelisk.

Members of the society hoped that the start of construction would make people become more interested in the project. Raising money for the structure with nothing more than a drawing had been difficult. The society thought that once people saw a real monument being built, they would want to contribute to its **funding**.

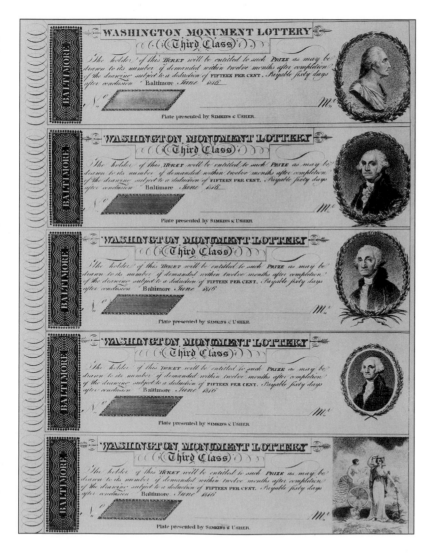

Raising money for monuments was difficult. Years earlier, during construction of the Washington Monument in Baltimore, lottery tickets were sold. The proceeds were used to build the monument.

## MAKING PROGRESS

Although many things about the monument were undecided, one thing was clear—its location. Congress had set aside 37 acres (15 ha) of free land for this purpose. Located near the White House, the site seemed ideal. It was also close to the Potomac River, which added to the monument's beauty. The river also provided an excellent means for shipping stones and other building materials to the construction site.

**The Washington Monument would be close to the White House, shown here around 1850.**

Blossoming cherry trees provide a colorful, scenic backdrop for the monument every spring.

Today, the Washington Monument is part of a nearly 2-mile (3-kilometer) stretch known as the National Mall. The Mall contains several monuments and memorials, as well as flower beds, pools, and fountains. The National Mall is also lined with two thousand American elm trees and three thousand cherry trees from Japan. Every spring, tourists come to the Mall to see the cherry trees blossom.

The society was pleased with the site. One of its members wrote, "[It] presents a beautiful view of the Potomac [River] . . . and is so elevated that the monument will be seen from all parts of the surrounding country." He also noted that "[It] would be in full view of Mount Vernon, where rests the ashes of the chief."

Digging at the monument's site began on April 18, 1848. Robert Mills was paid $500 per year to supervise the construction. Huge blocks of stone were needed just to get the monument's foundation started. Some of the blocks weighed as much as 8 tons (7.3 metric tons).

By summer, it was time to lay the structure's **cornerstone**. This event was planned for July 4, 1848, because George Washington himself was a great patriot. It was an event no one in the capital would soon forget. A crowd of more than twenty thousand people gathered for the ceremony. President James K. Polk was among the guests there that day, as were numerous Supreme Court justices and members of Congress. The crowd also included schoolchildren, firefighters, teachers, storeowners, barbers, clerks, and many other people.

The event was sponsored by the Freemasons, an international organization to which Washington had belonged. Many important Americans, including Benjamin Franklin, John Hancock, and Paul Revere, had also been Freemasons. The group was proud to play a role in honoring one of its most outstanding members. As someone remarked that day in a speech, "No more Washingtons shall come in our time . . . but his virtues are stamped on the heart of mankind."

It was a glorious day, and the monument seemed to be off to a terrific start. Anyone attending the ceremony might have thought this tall tribute to the nation's first president

GEN. GEO. WASHINGTON.

LAYING CORNER STONE, WASHINGTON MONUMENT.

Thousands of people gathered to celebrate the laying of the monument's cornerstone on July 4, 1848.

would be built in no time. Yet it didn't happen that way. Construction continued for the next six years, but then stopped. The Washington National Monument Society was out of money.

Construction on the monument continued steadily for about six years.

# PROBLEMS ALONG THE WAY

The society asked the government for money to help it complete the monument. Things began to look brighter when Congress agreed to set aside $200,000 for the work. Congress later took back the offer, however, just one night before the funds were delivered.

The trouble began after the society requested that every state contribute a stone for the monument's inner walls. This meant that the whole country would be represented within the monument. In addition to the states, foreign countries, religious organizations, business groups, American Indian tribes, and social clubs were encouraged to add stones as well. This practice got more people involved and helped spread the cost of the expensive stone blocks over many different groups.

Then trouble arose with the construction project. Ideally, no one was to be barred from helping with the construction of the monument. Some **prejudiced** people, however, wanted certain groups to be left out. Many of these individuals were members of a political party called the Know-Nothings. The Know-Nothings especially disliked

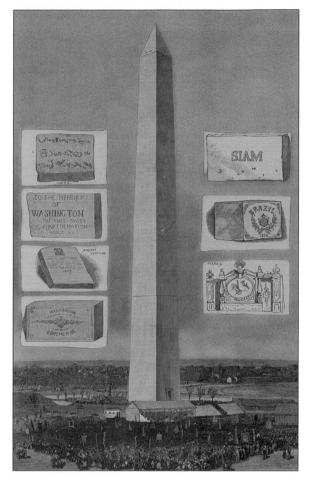

Stones from various organizations, as well as the states, were also used in the monument's construction.

## DONATED STONES

The Washington Monument contains a total of 193 donated stones from various sources. These stones decorate the east and west interior walls of the monument. Alaska provided a magnificent jade stone that is worth several million dollars today.

## THE KNOW-NOTHINGS

The Know-Nothing Party's official name was the American Party. While it claimed to represent "true Americans," it was a party whose beliefs were based on fear and prejudice. Because many of its activities were illegal, its members often had to act secretly. When asked about their plans, members were told to say that they "knew nothing." As a result, the party became commonly known as the Know-Nothing Party.

**immigrants** and Catholics. They did not want these people to be involved in the monument's construction.

These feelings came to a head in 1854, when Pope Pius IX donated a block of marble to the monument. The pope is the head of the Catholic Church, and the Know-Nothings were not pleased with his gift. On March 6, 1854, the Know-Nothings stole the Pope's stone from the shed at the monument's construction site. They either destroyed it or threw it into the Potomac River.

The Know-Nothings wanted to take control of the monument's construction so that immigrants and Catholics would not be involved in building it. They launched an effort to take over the Washington National Monument Society. Through a fixed election held on February 21, 1855, the Know-Nothings seized the organization's leadership. They remained in power for several years.

This nighttime meeting of the Know-Nothings took place in City Hall Park in Manhattan in 1855.

During the war, the monument's grounds were used for more practical purposes. At first, the area became a drill field for Union soldiers. Later, cattle grazed there to supply beef for Union troops.

With the Know-Nothings in charge, all the Catholics and immigrants working at the site were fired. The society's fund-raising efforts were then directed only at "genuine" Americans. To the Know-Nothings, this meant white Protestants who had been born in the United States. The monument's progress and quality suffered during this time. Poor-quality marble was used in the construction, and many stones had to be replaced later. Unable to raise enough money to continue construction, the Know-Nothings began to lose control of the project. In 1858, they withdrew from the project altogether. The original society members took charge once again.

Yet work on the monument did not resume right away. When the Civil War broke out in 1861, people became preoccupied with the crisis at hand. The unfinished obelisk would remain at less than one-third of its original height for some time to come.

In 1866, President Andrew Johnson encouraged society members to continue work on the monument.

## CONTINUING CONSTRUCTION

After the Civil War was over, interest in the monument stirred again. As President Andrew Johnson told members of the Washington National Monument Society in 1866, "Let us restore the Union and let us proceed with the monument as its symbol until it shall contain the pledge of all the states of the Union!" A decade later, in 1876—the one-hundredth anniversary of the signing of the Declaration of Independence—Americans were finally ready to act. Congress again promised to put aside $200,000 to help finish the structure. By then it had been under construction for more than twenty years.

Nevertheless, there were still some important questions to be answered before the project could go forward. The society had never settled on the final design for the monument. Some people thought completing the obelisk would be enough. Others argued that the obelisk was simply too "little . . . to be proud of." Before Robert Mills died in 1855, he stressed the importance of keeping the temple-styled building and colonnade. Otherwise, he warned that the monument was in danger of looking like "a stalk of asparagus."

On the one-hundredth anniversary of the signing of the Declaration of Independence, feelings of patriotism were high as people once again prepared to honor George Washington.

So, for a second time, the call went out for artists and architects to submit designs for the structure. Many new ideas came in. The society and Congress, which were then working together on the project, seriously considered five designs. The best of these was believed to have come from an American sculptor named William Wetmore Story. Story had worked and studied in Italy and was familiar with architectural styles abroad.

Story wanted to keep the monument's obelisk, but he had changes in mind for it. He hoped to surround the structure with an outer layer of marble. This new exterior was to be highly decorative. Story also wanted to change the monument's top. Instead of the nearly flat top that Mills had originally designed, Story wanted the structure to rise to a pyramid-shaped peak. The society liked Story's ideas. It said that his plan for the monument was "vastly superior in artistic taste and beauty" to the others that had been submitted.

However, as it turned out, parts of Story's proposed redesign involved some construction changes that the society was not willing to make. To use all his ideas, more than 40 feet (12 m) of the existing monument would have to be torn down and rebuilt. The fancy new exterior would also have added more weight to the monument than it could support.

In the end, it was determined that the obelisk built to honor George Washington would take a classically Egyptian form. It would be 555 feet (170 m) tall and **unadorned**, with the pyramid-shaped top that Story designed. At the time, there was wide public interest in the ancient ruins of Egypt. There, obelisks had been built to guard sacred temples from about 17 B.C. to A.D. 14. Many people admired the simple beauty of these structures.

An obelisk stands guard at the Temple of Amun in Egypt.

# BUILDING CHALLENGES

Meanwhile, Congress ordered work on the obelisk to continue, and construction started again in 1879. The task of building the monument then fell to Lieutenant Colonel Thomas L. Casey of the United States Army Corps of Engineers. The newly redesigned monument would still be quite massive. It was up to Casey to make sure that the foundation was both large and strong enough to support the structure.

Lt. Colonel Thomas L. Casey directed construction of the monument from 1879 until its completion in 1884.

This proved to be quite an undertaking. Casey had to create a second foundation that was two-and-a-half times larger than the first. Although the original foundation had been sound, the monument's new design required changes to its foundation.

The new foundation went down 13.5 feet (4.1 m) deeper into the ground than the first foundation did. That meant a new cornerstone had to be laid because the first was then buried beneath the soil. The second cornerstone was laid on August 7, 1880, at the 150-foot (45.7-m) level, where building would resume. President Rutherford B. Hayes, along with several

**The monument's foundation was strengthened to hold the additional weight of the new structure.**

government officials, laid the monument's second corner-stone in a small, quiet ceremony.

Casey worked hard to complete the monument. He removed the poor-quality marble the Know-Nothings had

**This photograph clearly shows the change in stone color halfway up the monument.**

added to the structure. That reduced the obelisk to a height of about 150 feet (45.7 m). In ordering new marble stones, Casey tried to match the older ones exactly. He specified that these "must be white, strong, sound . . . and must in texture and color so conform to the marble now built in the monument as not to present any marked or striking contrast . . ." Unfortunately, this wasn't possible. Although Casey found the high-quality marble he wanted, he was not able to find the ideal color match. The monument had been started decades earlier, and matching stones were no longer available. Casey did his best, but a distinct color change can be seen above 150 feet (45.7 m) on the monument.

Completing the monument required a good deal of work. Slowly, Casey made headway. In time, he had the monument's inner iron framework in place. The framework helps hold the monument up. Produced by a Pennsylvania company, this structural piece was firmly secured to the inner stones. Meanwhile, the monument continued to grow taller. By August 1884, the Washington Monument stood 500 feet (152 m) tall.

Then, only the final phase of construction remained— the completion of the monument's top. On December 6, 1884, workers placed a 3,300-pound (1,498-kilogram) marble capstone (top stone) on the monument. The stone's point was removed and replaced with a solid **aluminum**, pyramid-shaped cap. It was the first time aluminum had been used in American architecture. The metal pyramid

★ ★ ★ ★

housed a lightning rod to protect the structure during storms. On the east side of the aluminum pyramid, the Latin phrase *laus deo* is inscribed. It means "praise be to God."

**Two stonecutters work on the capstone of the Washington Monument.**

36

On December 6, 1884, workers placed the capstone and a pyramid of cast aluminum on top of the monument, completing construction.

## THE CROWN JEWEL

The aluminum cap on the Washington Monument is a great source of pride to the aluminum industry. Before the cap was selected for use on the monument, many people didn't even know what aluminum was. The fact that it was among the materials chosen for such an important structure served as a boost to the aluminum industry as a whole. Aluminum was a precious metal at the time, and the cap was treated like a jewel. It was displayed for the public at Tiffany & Co. jewelers in New York City before being placed on the structure.

# THE GRAND OPENING

February 21, 1885, was the proud day of the monument's formal dedication. It was a cold day, and there was snow on the ground, but that did not stop people from attending the ceremony. President Chester A. Arthur, who looked chilly even in his fur-lined coat, spoke fondly of the monument. Other officials addressed the audience as well. But perhaps the most meaningful words came from Lieutenant Colonel Thomas L. Casey. At the end of his speech, he turned to President Arthur and said, "For and in behalf of the joint commission for the completion of the Washington Monument, I deliver you this column." The monument that had taken thirty-six years to build was finally finished.

As part of the celebration, there was a magnificent fireworks display in the nation's capital that night. One of the displays looked like George Washington on his horse. It lit up the sky as a glowing reminder of the outstanding patriot for whom the monument had been built.

The Washington Monument's story doesn't end there. Since its opening, visitors from around the world have come to see the Washington Monument. A short elevator ride has brought countless guests to the monument's observation

President Chester A. Arthur made a speech at the dedication ceremony.

Photos of the monument reflected in the pool are a popular tourist item.

## FACTS ABOUT THE WASHINGTON MONUMENT

• The total cost of the Washington Monument was $1,187,710.

• The Washington Monument is 555 feet, 5 -1/8 inches (170 m) tall. That's equal to the height of about thirty giraffes placed on top of one another.

• The Washington Monument weighs 90,854 tons (82,421 metric tons), about equal to the weight of seven male African elephants.

• There are 36,491 blocks of granite and marble in the monument.

• The thickness of the monument's walls at its base is 15 feet (4.5 m), but its walls taper to just 18 inches (45 centimeters) toward the top.

• 896 steps lead to the top of the monument, but these were permanently closed to the public in 1976. This was done to limit wear and tear on the monument.

• The Washington Monument was the tallest building on Earth until France's Eiffel Tower was built in 1889. The Eiffel Tower is 1,063 feet (324 m) tall, making it about 508 feet (155 m) taller than the Washington Monument.

• The fifty flags surrounding the Washington Monument's base represent the fifty states of the Union.

• The Washington Monument is the National Mall's oldest memorial to a president.

• The image of the Washington Monument is reflected in a pool called the Reflecting Pool. Located between the Washington Monument and the Lincoln Memorial, the pool holds 6,750,000 gallons (25,548,750 liters) of water.

From the top of the monument, visitors can get a good view of the surrounding area.

In 1999, scaffolding surrounded the monument as workers made repairs.

room at the 500-foot (152-m) level. From there, they can look out over all of Washington, D.C., and beyond.

Over the years, the effects of weathering and daily wear and tear caused by visitors took its toll on the towering structure. Experts warned that some of the exterior stones were beginning to chip, and pieces were starting to flake off. On rainy days, the structure had even begun to leak, damaging some of the interior stones.

Something had to be done before the situation got worse. Some **restoration** of the monument was undertaken in 1934 and 1964, but it was not enough. As a highly valued national symbol, the monument needed to be protected and preserved. In the late 1990s, a great effort was made to restore the Washington Monument to its former glory.

The restoration cost more than $9.4 million. It was sponsored by a partnership between government and private sources. Restoring the monument would take several years.

During that time, chipped and patched stones were repaired and cracks were sealed where necessary.

New mortar replaced the old in many spots, and thousands of feet of interior walls were given a thorough cleaning. Some observation windows were resealed, and eight new warning lights were installed to protect aircraft as well as the monument from a collision. The heating and cooling systems as well as the elevators were improved. Other repairs to preserve the monument were also completed.

On February 22, 2002, a ceremony was held to celebrate both the completion of the restoration and the 270th anniversary of George Washington's birth. Maryland Representative Roscoe G. Bartlett spoke at the event. He noted that "George Washington was a giant among the many giants of our nation's founders and the single most **indispensable** individual responsible for America's success." With the restoration complete, the nation has shown that it still remembers and respects this great American. His monument once again stands as a worthy tribute to him.

To help celebrate the reopening of the monument in 2002, the Old Guard Fife and Drum Corps dressed in historic costumes and entertained visitors with music.

# Glossary

**aluminum**—a silver-white soft metal

**architect**—person trained to design and oversee the construction of buildings

**chariot**—a cart with two wheels that is drawn by horses

**complex**—made up of separate yet related parts

**cornerstone**—a stone in a large and important building that is usually carved with a date

**funding**—money for a project

**immigrants**—people entering a country other than their own to live permanently

**indispensable**—absolutely necessary

**memorial**—structure or statue built in memory of someone

**mourning**—expressing sadness and grief over a loss

**patriotism**—love for one's country

**prejudiced**—having a belief or attitude (usually negative) about someone based on that person's race, religion, or other characteristics

**restoration**—the act of repairing something to return it to its original condition

**tribute**—something done to show admiration or respect

**unadorned**—not decorated

**unanimously**—having the agreement of everyone

# Timeline: The Washington

| 1783 | 1799 | 1833 | 1836 | 1848 | 1854 | 1855 |
|------|------|------|------|------|------|------|

**The Continental Congress proposes that a statue of George Washington on a horse be built.**

American-born architect Robert Mills wins the design contest sponsored by the Washington National Monument Society.

Work on the monument begins. The cornerstone is laid on July 4.

George Washington dies.

The Washington National Monument Society is formed.

The Know-Nothings throw a memorial stone for the monument donated by Pope Pius IX into the Potomac River.

The Know-Nothings seize control of the Washington National Monument Society.

# Monument

**1861** The Civil War breaks out, and work on the monument temporarily stops.

**1879** Construction on the monument resumes.

**1880** The monument's second cornerstone is laid on August 7.

**1884** The 3,300-pound (1,498-kg) marble capstone is placed on the monument on December 6.

**1885** The monument's formal dedication is held on February 21.

**1998–2000** The monument undergoes an extensive renovation.

**2002** A ceremony is held to celebrate the completion of the restoration and the 270th anniversary of George Washington's birth.

# To Find Out More

## BOOKS AND JOURNALS

Ashabranner, Brent K. *The Washington Monument: A Beacon for America*. New Milford, Conn.: Twenty-First Century Books, 2002.

Curlee, Lynn. *Capital*. New York: Atheneum, 2003.

Harness, Cheryl. *George Washington*. Washington, D.C.: National Geographic Society, 2000.

Heilbroner, Joan. *Meet George Washington*. New York: Random House, 2001.

January, Brendan. *The National Mall*. Danbury, Conn.: Children's Press, 2000.

Mello, Tara Baukus. *George Washington: First U.S. President*. Broomall, Penn.: Chelsea House, 2000.

## ONLINE SITES

Washington Monument Home Page
*http://www.nps.gov/wamo/home.htm*

Historic Valley Forge
*http://www.ushistory.org/valleyforge/*

# Index

Bold numbers indicate illustrations.

47

# About the Author

Award-winning children's book author **Elaine Landau** worked as a newspaper reporter, a children's book editor, and a youth services librarian before becoming a full-time writer. She has written more than two hundred books for young readers. Landau has a bachelor's degree in English and journalism from New York University and a master's degree in library and information science from Pratt Institute. She lives in Miami, Florida, with her husband, Norman, and her son, Michael.